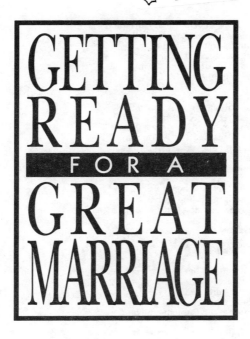

GETTING READY FOR A GREAT MARRIAGE

R. PAUL STEVENS

NAVPRESS
A MINISTRY OF THE NAVIGATORS
P.O. BOX 6000, COLORADO SPRINGS, COLORADO 80934

The Navigators is an international Christian
organization. Jesus Christ gave His followers
the Great Commission to go and make
disciples (Matthew 28:19). The aim of The
Navigators is to help fulfill that commission by multiplying laborers for Christ in
every nation.

NavPress is the publishing ministry of The
Navigators. NavPress publications are tools
to help Christians grow. Although publications alone cannot make disciples or change
lives, they can help believers learn biblical
discipleship, and apply what they learn to
their lives and ministries.

© 1990 by R. Paul Stevens
All rights reserved, including translation
Library of Congress Catalog Card Number:
   90-60970
ISBN 08910-92927

Cover photo: Chuck Kuhn

Printed in the United States of America

Contents

Author

R. Paul Stevens is the Academic Dean of Regent College in Vancouver, British Columbia, Canada. With his wife, Gail, he leads marriage enrichment and spiritual friendship weekends for married couples. Now that all three of their children are married, Paul and Gail spend part of each year serving the Church in developing countries, currently in Kenya.

Paul has three degrees, including a D.Min. from Fuller Seminary. Over twenty-five years in pastoral work and teaching are the background for this volume. His other books are *Liberating the Laity* (InterVarsity Press), *Married for Good* (IVP), *Marriage Spirituality* (IVP), and several Bible study guides.

Paul and Gail love to spend time alone at their tiny seaside cabin, which is mentioned in this book.

1

Why Not Marry for Good?

"Do you think we will make it? With one in three marriages ending in divorce, do you think Jim and I will become a statistic?"

Jim and Sally had arrived at the home of Bob and Sheila Stewart for their second premarital counseling session. In their church, each engaged couple is carefully assigned to a trained volunteer couple, who gives several months of couple-to-couple friendship. When the four were comfortably seated in front of the fireplace, Sally revealed what was troubling her.

"When my mom divorced my father, I saw firsthand how hurtful it was for everyone in the family. And frankly, I would rather not marry unless I can be absolutely sure that we will never become a statistic."

Not every engaged couple can verbalize this deep fear of failure as well as Sally did. It is a fear that erodes one's ability to make an unconditional covenant. Marriage, according to God's design, is not a *contract* in which each party agrees to exchange goods and services according to previously arranged conditions. For some, marriage is an agreement to meet each other's emotional and sexual needs, to make each other happy, or to exchange "breadwinning" for domestic service and raising children. In contrast, marriage was intended to be a *covenant* in which two people belong together "for better, for worse, for richer, for poorer, in sickness and in health, until death do us part."

Marriage is a lifelong covenant partnership, solemnly made before God, in which a man and a woman agree to belong to each other as long as they both shall live. Such a covenant should be witnessed by family and friends and acknowledged by the state. God, in a way we don't fully understand, enters into the marriage covenant and blesses it.

Marriage is not a contract for happiness but a covenant of belonging, and it results in something better than happiness: maturity, intimacy, and the birth of real love. *Commitment* is an often-heard word today, but *covenant* is more relevant to marital success. When commitment breaks down, the marriage covenant, like huge divine hands, holds a couple together when they can no longer hold each other. We were designed to be caught by the covenant when commitment wears thin. At such times, when we have trouble keeping our vows, our vows keep us.

I once built a little seaside cabin without thinking about the need for a proper foundation. And so I had to build the foundation after the building was up. This is better than not building a foundation at all! But it is better still to build the foundation before the building is constructed. Likewise, in marriage, it is best to build a covenant before you work on fine tuning the relationship.

So if you are thinking of marriage, this book will help

you explore together the lost art of getting married for good. I have two goals: to increase your capability of making a covenant and to help you discern your covenant readiness.

"Yes, Sally. You can be sure you will never become a statistic. If you prepare well for marriage, you can make those vows with no reservation, knowing to whom you make them. Our covenant God will be with you as you do so. And you *can* be married for good—forever."

2

The Divorceless Covenant

If one in three Ford cars collapsed on the highway, someone would check to see if those cars were being made according to the original design. In this book we will explore God's original design for marriage. Marriages are collapsing all around us. Let's see what the Creator originally had in mind.

Most people think a successful marriage depends on good conflict resolution and communication skills. These are important, but they will not save a marriage if there is no covenant.

Contrary to what many people think, marriages today are probably of a higher quality than those of our parents. We are working harder on companionship skills than ever before. But most marriages lack stability, without which they simply won't last. No one can keep one's marriage fine tuned every hour of the day. Every marriage has a season of "for worse." But the "for worse" season can become "for better" if the marriage is founded on a divorce-proof covenant.

One of the saddest realities in the Western world

today is that people are entering marriage with the thought that they can leave it. They make a contract, not a covenant. When they say their vows, they retain an emotional loophole "in case it doesn't work out." In so doing, they make a conditional agreement to be husband and wife, instead of a covenant for life.

Our society discourages long-term commitments. If the future is unthinkable, so is the promise "till death do us part." Lacking the security of a covenant, a marriage relationship is as vulnerable as the health of that partnership at any given moment. In contrast, the covenant gives a couple the security to dare to confront, to work through problems rather than around them. They can count on the relationship to survive. The marriage itself can be perennially renewed.

The word *covenant* takes us to the heart of the Bible's message. God entered into a solemn covenant with His people Israel, and Christ does also with His bride, the Church. In Scripture we read, "So you will be my people, and I will be your God" (Jeremiah 30:22). Those words express the heart of our bondedness with God. Our relationship with Him is a covenant of belonging, not a contract for mutual service. Christ does not say, "I will give you eternal salvation if you give Me a lifetime of sacrificial service." Rather, Christ says simply, "I am yours, and you are Mine. I will never divorce you."

Marriage is the great human analogy for what the Apostle Paul calls the "mystery" of Christ's relationship to His people (Ephesians 5:25-32). Hosea was the first biblical writer to explain God's covenant with His people by using marriage as an analogy. For Hosea the analogy worked both ways. God's marriage to unfaithful Israel inspired Hosea to keep and renew his relationship with his unfaithful wife, Gomer. At the same time, Hosea's own marriage experience became a window through which he could see and respond to the heart of the covenant-making God, *Yahweh*.

Building a marriage is like building a house. You start with the foundation, which in this case means forming a covenant. So in the chapters ahead—some have short exercises for you to do—we will explore your readiness to build the marriage house. But first we must ask why you want to build that house.

3

The Myth of Marriage for Love

O nce in a while I ask my wife, Gail, why she married me. After twenty-five years of marriage, that is a dangerous question to ask. If she is in a playful mood, she might look at the light reflected from the top of my head and say, "I was attracted by the wavy hair you once had." But she will also say that she liked the way I treated people; she found me challenging but not domineering; she felt comfortable with me; she felt she fitted well with my family.

"It was your mother's cooking," I will respond to the same question. "I was a hungry student, and your mom's barbequed chicken was irresistible. And your dad knew more theology than my professors." But I had better reasons for marrying Gail. I felt comfortable with her—totally comfortable. I did not need to pretend I was someone else. She brought out the best in me, like a fan blowing on the coals of my life.

Those were our conscious thoughts. But unconsciously, we both had deep longings and needs that were hard to verbalize. When preparing for marriage, you will discover that those hidden facts turn out to be even more important than the feeling of love.

One persistent myth is that people marry because of love. In reality, the coming together of two people in marriage is something like a twin-headed iceberg. Above the water we see what looks like two icebergs. But below the water is one iceberg, nine-tenths of which is hidden. On the surface two people say to each other "I love you. I want to marry you." But underneath are powerful forces driving them toward marriage.

For instance, some marry out of rebellion. "As I went down the aisle," a young lady confessed, "I knew I had won!"

"Won what?" I asked innocently.

"The battle against my father," she said. "He said my marriage would not last, and I was determined, just this once, to have the final word." But she lost the argument with her dad—and her husband. Some couples marry just to get out of their parents' houses.

Peer pressure drives some to marriage. It is hard not to marry, even half-heartedly, when most of one's graduating class is doing so.

Loneliness and self-pity are also poor reasons to get married. Perhaps worse is marrying to end someone else's misery. A friend of mine told me he married his bride to see if he could make her happy. She was deeply hurt during the war years in Germany and hardly ever smiled. He had hoped to bring her to life, but he never did. And their marriage did not thrive. Marriage does not add a magic ingredient to the personalities of the partners. Pity the couple who marries for pity!

Sometimes a man or woman is so angry at being cast off by a sweetheart that he or she plunges into another relationship on the rebound. Others want a beauty queen, a domestic servant, or a parental substitute. What is so tragic is that many people are unaware of those below-the-surface reasons for wanting a spouse.

Psychiatrists know that men and women sometimes pick a spouse whom they hope will capture lost elements in their own childhood. They want a partner who will make up for what they missed at home. Often this results in re-creating the tragedy of their own upbringing. If one wants to be a child in relation to the other, the spouse who is required to be a parent will become frustrated with the partner who refuses to grow up. This hurt will turn to anger, and anger to fighting. A skillful counselor can help them, but it is far better to deal with this problem before marriage than after.

When two people are friends long enough, in enough different contexts, the poor reasons for marriage often surface without the help of a professional counselor. In a long premarital friendship, in which everything is discussed, everything is known, two people can deal with the less-than-adequate reasons for marriage, and then build on the right reasons. There are *right* reasons to marry.

4

The Right Reasons for Marrying

M any marriages fail today not because people expect too little of marriage but because they expect too much. They come with an empty bowl saying, "I need security; I need affection; I need life-direction; I need solace and encouragement; I need an identity; I need to know who I am. I come with my empty bowl to you, for you are a wonderful person. I know you can fill it right up." But before long the partner says, "It just so happens I have an empty bowl too." So you exchange empty bowls until you realize your marriage is not based on a strong foundation.

Choosing a marriage partner is not like choosing a new dress or a new car. It is not simply a case of getting "the best we can." The Bible speaks of marriage as a calling, a vocation (Genesis 2:22, Matthew 19:6, 1 Corinthians 7:17). It does this partly because God takes initiatives in our relationships. While some of the hidden reasons for marriage come from our dark side, God is working within us, calling forth the best in us.

In Genesis 2, our Creator God is pictured as the

Father of the bride, bringing Eve to the waiting Adam. God is also at work in each potential marriage relationship, whether we are aware of it or not, through the needs and longings He has planted in our hearts.

We are capable of companionship with the other sex. God said concerning the first marriage described in the history of the world, "It is not good for the man to be alone" (Genesis 2:18). So He created a helper-partner who was equal to but different from the man. We are created with a longing for the other sex, not merely to satisfy the sex drive but also to fulfill an appetite for intimacy. Short-term disposable relationships cannot satisfy this desire.

We also were created with a need for intimacy. But intimacy is not something you get through therapy sessions or by exploring another person's body. It is the fruit of a lifetime of belonging to one other person.

Marriage is also an invitation to grow up, to become more mature. Martin Luther once said that God has given two institutions for our sanctification: the family and the Church. Today many couples prefer not to have children because becoming a parent means that they themselves must stop being children and accept adult responsibilities. Few children understand that they are helping their parents grow up!

The marriage covenant is also a great place to learn how to love. To love is to put your partner's needs before your own. It is not, as someone has said, "a feeling that you are going to get a feeling you never felt before." Rather, to love is to make an unconditional commitment to an imperfect person. Many people marry not *to* love but to *be loved.* Before long they say something like this: "Our relationship no longer satisfies my needs."

Love is of such grandeur that it can never be experienced in a one-night stand, a fleeting passion, or an arms-length arrangement. Love is at its best in the context of a relationship in which the key to the lock that padlocks you together has been thrown away. Then, instead of finding yourself in a relational prison, you accept it as a garden in which to cultivate freedom, personhood, and maturity. God made marriage irrevocable for love's sake—His own and ours. I think that is why, in the Genesis account, God Himself is the Matchmaker.

A SHORT EXERCISE

Write the answers to these questions while you are alone. Then share them with your friend.

◆ God brings people together through their healthy needs. Why is it not good for you to be alone? (See Genesis 2:18.)
◆ What needs have brought you to this place of considering lifelong partnership?
◆ What needs cannot be met by another human being and must be met through relationship with God?
◆ God allowed Adam to name all the other creatures (Genesis 2:19-20) that he might realize his need for a suitable partner. What longings has God put in your heart that have not yet been met by anyone else?
◆ Why do you think those longings may be partially met by your friend?

5

The Divine Matchmaker

"Matchmaker, Matchmaker, make me a match; find me a find, catch me a catch. Matchmaker, Matchmaker, look through your book. And make me a perfect match."[1]

One of the most dangerous things to say or think once you are married is this: "Getting married to you was a big mistake." The time to consider this possibility is before, not after.

Once you are married, God Himself will cooperate with your every effort to give your marriage both quality and stability. God does not rejoice in loveless, empty covenants. When He made a covenant with His people, He did so for the purpose of mutual blessing. He has the same desire for marriage. He wants husbands and wives to bless each other.

God is involved in this process from the beginning. He is the Father of the bride *and* the groom, the One who arranges the match.

The Genesis account (2:18-25) gives us a graphic description of God's secret work in the hearts of Adam and Eve. God created a hunger in Adam for a companion by pronouncing judgment on his loneliness: "It is not good for the man to be alone" (2:18). God formed other creatures and brought them to the man to let him express relationship with them by naming them. In doing so, the man had dominion over the fish of the sea, the birds of the air, and over every living creature (1:28). But Adam needed a creature he could name, as a companion to himself. This special "other" would share his dominion over everything in creation.

The narrative is full of the initiative of the Divine Matchmaker: "I will make a helper suitable for him" (2:18). "The LORD God caused the man to fall into a deep sleep" (2:21). Figuratively speaking of this literal event, Adam was as good as dead as a solitary person. While Adam slept, God "took one of the man's ribs" (2:21) and made a woman. Then, as though He were the Father of the bride, God "brought her to the man" (2:22).

The Bible describes people getting married in all kinds of ways. Some couples were matched up by parents, others had a romantic relationship, some met through the initiative of trusted and godly friends, and in at least one instance a sinful sexual adventure ended in marriage. Yet God took even poor marriages, or marriages for wrong reasons, and made them constructive. Therefore we should neither despair nor presume.

We should not despair, because God can take even our foolish decisions and weave them into His great purpose. The only ultimate mistake is not to want to do His will. But neither should we presume. Feeling "in love" is no guarantee that a proposed marriage is therefore blessed by God and initiated by God. There is more to living out a calling than feeling good about it.

The Christian Church maintains that marriage is a

calling. To be "called" means simply that you cannot now live for yourself alone or look exclusively for your own fulfillment in the relationship. Called persons are chosen for a greater purpose than their own personal happiness. In Christian marriage happiness is the byproduct of seeking something even greater than happiness.

So the true Father of the bride and groom is God Himself, not the sex drive, or social expectations, or manipulating and scheming parents. Marriages are usually arranged by God. That is our ultimate hope and, at the same time, the secret meaning of the words of Jesus: "Therefore what God has joined together, let man not separate" (Mark 10:9). These are the most searching words on marriage in the New Testament. They are surely not written merely for Christians. Jesus declares by those solemn and liberating words that couples entering into marriage have not taken marriage upon themselves. They are responding to God's call. They do this in the nitty gritty of their courtship and friendship as well as in the solitude of their own prayers.

NOTE
1. "Matchmaker" (from *Fiddler on the Roof*). Words by Sheldon Harnick, music by Jerry Bock. Copyright © 1964 by Alley Music Corporation and Trio Music Company, Inc. All rights administered by Hudson Bay Music, Inc. International copyright secured. Made in U.S.A. All rights reserved. Used by permission.

A SHORT EXERCISE

◆ God brings a couple together partly through what we call circumstances. Your life is not a bundle of accidents. How was it more than chance that you met your friend?

◆ What other circumstances suggest that God has participated in the forming of your relationship?

◆ When Adam was presented with Eve, he uttered the first poetry in the Bible, the first song of praise. He literally exclaimed, "At last" (Genesis 2:23). It is a cry of relational joy and worship. "This is now [or, at last] bone of my bones and flesh of my flesh; she shall be called 'woman,' for she was taken out of man" (2:23). Adam saw that Eve was like him but different, different but suitable, suitable but mysterious, mysterious but knowable. They fit together. How in your relationship do you feel made for each other?

◆ In what way could you say that you are more yourself with your future partner than without?

6

When the Infatuation Wears Off

"When a girl marries, she exchanges the attention of many men for the inattention of one."[1] This cynical statement was made by Helen Rowland. It reminds us that courting is as important after marriage as before. So a good time to learn is now!

In our society, dating, or "going out" as it is sometimes called, is the context in which we learn to court. But courting has become both a lost art and a lost word. The old English word *woo* means to plead for the response of another person's heart. Wooing involves opening up another's heart to a love relationship. It is passionate but not possessive, persuasive but not pushy. You may not realize that the Bible tells us how to go about the delightful work of developing a relationship that leads to marriage. But before I explore that, I have a confession to make.

Gail was not the first person I ever dated. I had my first special time with a person of the opposite sex, besides my mother, when I was in the fourth grade. I lied to my mom and dad and told them I was going to a special event downtown with my best male friend. When I got to the children's theater, I met my special girlfriend from school.

So I have had a long history of courting. I treasure all my dating relationships because they gave me an appreciation of each person's specialness. Also, with each relationship, I grew and discovered what kind of person I am and what kind of person I wanted to marry. Still, I am well aware of the deficiencies of the dating system in our society.

The dating game is too frequently a staged play in which each person presents an attractive public self to a string of "others." Before revealing their private selves, dating couples often get entangled sexually on the second or third date. They believe that touch, feel, and fondle are quick ways to intimacy. But these ways shut off conversation, thereby preventing the couple from knowing each other, sometimes until it is too late.

John projects the image of the macho male, but inside he is insecure. Mary is gorgeous and alluring in her public self, but privately she feels she is a nobody. The needy inner self in each person falls in love with the attractive outer self in the other in an attempt to meet a personal need. The two are fascinated with each other's personages.

If two people like this marry before the infatuation wears off, they may delay for two or three years the inevitable process of facing their own and their partner's faults. Psychologists call this a collective defense mechanism. When reality sets in, they will probably need professional help.

Some people say the greatest problem with marriage today is our practice of courtship. This is undoubtedly true, if courtship is defined as mutual infatuation and seduction. Only a long friendship can get people past that staged drama. Most people need a full year or more of in-depth friendship to make sure they are not simply infatuated.

Falling in love is considered by many social scientists an experience of temporary insanity. One literally goes out of one's mind. The word *infatuation* means deranged. But it doesn't seem that way to the person who experiences that delightful derangement.

Love takes time, lasts long, focuses on a suitable person, considers the whole person, and helps one to face reality and to tackle problems realistically. Infatuation comes suddenly, lasts briefly, often attaches to an unsuitable person, focuses on physical thrills, and disregards problems and barriers. Infatuation is a flight from reality into a wonderful romantic world. It cloaks the person one claims to love with a shroud of perfection. The beloved is ideal, but not real.

Courting does not have to lead to infatuation. A redeemed, God-honoring dating system can be one instrument of many that God might choose to help us find a life partner. If we reject this system, we must come up with something better. God does not usually send a marriage partner by special delivery. He graciously includes us in the process and expects us to take initiatives. It is how we go about finding a partner that matters.

NOTE
1. Helen Rowland, quoted in Maureen Baker, ed., *The Family: Changing Trends in Canada* (Toronto: McGraw Hill Ryerson Ltd., 1984), page 90.

7

The Lost Art of Courting

W hen I met Gail I felt our relationship was to be different from others I'd had. I am not saying that persons who have had only one dating relationship before marriage are unprepared to discern God's choice. But getting to know several people well by dating as a group, and by having special times alone with individuals, can be helpful. Women should be encouraged to take appropriate initiatives with men, without being stigmatized. Courting is not just a learned skill for men.

Courting, or dating, should be encouraged within the church. Often Christian men seem reticent to take initiatives to get to know female friends in special ways, or in a setting that might set tongues wagging. Perhaps they respect women too much to use them for personal gratification, as they see many men doing. Perhaps they have been delivered by Christ from a lustful past, but are still afraid of their own responses if left alone with an attractive woman. Or perhaps they just need the female version of courting—encouragement! Whatever the case, the Bible gives us a remarkable insight: Our God is not merely interested in romance; He *invented* it!

In the second chapter of Hosea, the Lord courts His bride, the people of God, and the prophet Hosea learns from the Master-Lover how to mend his broken relationship with his own wife, Gomer. By overhearing the Lord's conversation with Hosea, we are invited to learn how the Lord gives a warm, winning, and wise appeal to the heart of His own creatures. The Lord said, "I am now going to allure her; I will lead her into the desert and speak tenderly to her" (Hosea 2:14). There are two references here for courting: "allure" and "speak tenderly." (The Hebrew literally means "speak to the heart.")

Allure or its equivalent is almost always used in the Bible in a negative sense: for the seduction of a virgin in Exodus 22, and the enticing of Samson by Delilah in Judges 14. But in Hosea 2:16, *allure* has a positive meaning. There, *allure* means positive persuasion. As with all persuasion, alluring, or courting, can be dangerous. The godly courter will never persuade another person to suspend judgment or compromise morality.

Often a man is the first to take the initiative to establish a relationship. After all, God is the Husband; the Church is His bride. But biblical examples show how a woman may take sensitive initiatives to make the desires of her heart known.

The story of Ruth's "courting" Boaz is an example of a woman making herself attractive (Ruth 3:3), being available to a suitable marriage partner (3:7), and being specific about her relational interests (3:9). Some Christian women are so anxious about appearing forward that they fail to give the encouragement, the signals, and take the initiatives that are appreciated by a man who is shy.

Many women do not understand the courage it takes for a man to make a phone call to a woman he likes. Anxiety heightens when the line is busy. The whole project is called off when her sister answers the phone!

The second time I saw Gail, and before I had taken her out, she deliberately stopped as we were leaving a meeting and started talking to me. She expressed interest in me and encouraged me to take more initiative to get to know her. Each of us needs to feel special enough to be sought. The rest of our story gets even more dramatic. I cut a whole day of classes to secure the next meeting with her. Several months later, when she was traveling in Europe, an orchid delivered to her hotel room on her birthday apparently was worth much more to Gail than the little money it cost me. (Often, a woman knows quite early in the relationship how she feels about a man, but she may treasure this intuition until he has expressed his intention and desires.)

But remember, there is a second word in Hosea's prophecy that talks about courting or wooing. The Hebrew is usually translated simply as "speak tenderly." That word is used in Isaiah 40:2, where the prophet is called to woo the heart of Jerusalem with warm, winning speech.

Of all the words a prophet might use to bring God's message to His people, God sent Isaiah with the language a man might use to plead for a maiden's heart, knowing he has nothing to offer but his love, and trusting love will welcome him in return. Those were not words of mindless passion, because biblically the heart includes not only emotions but also thoughts, reason, and conscience. Such love-language takes into consideration the values and needs of the beloved other. It reflects a right kind of infatuation and speaks of being a bit crazy about someone. Frankly, we all need to use such terms especially after we are married.

If courtship is a warm, winning, and wise appeal to a person's heart, over a long period of time, allowing one to know their friend truly and respect him or her utterly, then we need more of it. And not just before marriage. If we learn courting well before marriage, we will have exchanged the attention of many for the continuing attention of one.

A SHORT EXERCISE

Just as God wanted to take His bride to a special place (the solitude of the desert), for a special time, to say special words and to do special things, so we need to learn the art of nonmanipulative courting. Finish the next four sentences and then share your answers with your friend.

◆ The special places I like to go with you are . . .
◆ The special times I feel most responsive to you are . . .
◆ The special words that mean the most to me when spoken by you are . . .
◆ The special acts that convince me of your love are . . .

8

Covenant Readiness

"There are two basic causes for trouble in marriage: not finding in marriage what one expected to find, and not expecting what one actually finds."[1]

Premarital counseling usually helps couples explore their expectations related to communication, in-laws, sex, money, vocation, and religion. This exercise of counseling gives couples a chance to recognize that not all of their expectations will be met by their partner and to be ready for some experiences they did not expect. Certainly this realization can be beneficial to newlyweds.

Marriages fail today not so much because couples expect too little of each other but because they expect too much. Such is the modern self-fulfilling, mutual need-meeting, bilateral contract called marriage. Marriage has become an idol, and ultimately every idol is a disappointment.

But what we will begin to do in this chapter is to shape our expectations around the demands of the covenant, not the covenant partner. To be ready to make a covenant is more important than to be capable of being a perfect or near-perfect husband or wife. God's original design in Genesis 2 has never been improved upon.

"Therefore what God has joined together" (Matthew 19:6) is not merely God's endorsement of a couple's decision to marry. Those words speak of God's secret conspiracy to join two people—whatever their religious or nonreligious persuasion—when they agree to make a covenant. To unpack the secret of this divine conspiracy is our task together.

God joins marriage partners, not ministers or justices of the peace or well-meaning couples. He is not only the Father of the bride but the Officiating Minister. And He joins people when they marry—as the old service put it—"as God's Word doth allow."

In referring to Genesis 2 (Matthew 19:3-6) Jesus takes us beyond culture into the paradise of God—the Garden of Eden. There we can discover God's untarnished model for marriage: a man and a woman joined in indissoluble unity. We read, "The man and his wife were both naked, and they felt no shame" (Genesis 2:25). Those words refer not merely to Adam and Eve's physical nakedness. Their selves were naked. There was no shame, no masks, no self-defense.

When two people become one, Jesus implied, they cannot become two again without mutilating what God has joined together. This is the first and final grounds for the statement that whoever enters marriage must renounce the possibility of leaving it.

Probably no one has explained the crucial sentence in Genesis 2:24 more simply and more profoundly than Walter Trobisch in his book *I Married You*.[2] Concentrating on the three key phrases, "leave," "cleave," and "one flesh," Trobisch helps us understand that the marriage covenant has a public part, leaving father and mother; a personal part, cleaving; and a private part, one flesh.

"Leaving" is symbolized by wedlock, that public act by which two people state they belong to each other in an exclusive relationship. "Cleaving" means the joining of two people in a friendship that will extend throughout their lives. "One flesh" is the fulfillment of the first two, when a couple expresses with their bodies the reality of leaving and cleaving.

The abiding absence of any one of the three parts of the covenant means there is no covenant at all. Covenant readiness must explore all three. We will start with the question, "Are you ready to leave home?"

NOTES
1. Norman Wright, *Marital Counseling* (San Francisco: Harper & Row, 1981), page 1.
2. Walter Trobisch, *I Married You* (New York: Harper & Row, 1971).

o

9

Ready to Leave Home

M any men and women think they have left home because they have moved to a college dorm or an apartment. But leaving home is more than transferring residence. It involves transferring one's primary human loyalty from the family of origin to a newly created family of husband and wife.

More than that, leaving home means being released from hurtful and sick family patterns learned in one's family of origin. It is not uncommon, for instance, for a forty-year-old father to seek his mother's approval for the way he raises her grandchildren, even though this means siding with his mother rather than his wife.

To leave home emotionally is hard. Communication patterns learned in one's childhood are like tape-recorded messages waiting to be played when the right button is pushed by a spouse. Sometimes a person's real father is not as bad as the tape-recorded parent stored deep in one's brain.

Whether they leave home in a huff, are kicked out, go to college as a convenient escape, or happily stay at home until the day they are married with full parental blessing, many men and women never leave home emotionally. They transfer their need to be approved by their parents to their spouses. Sick relationships in the home are repeated generation to generation unless insight and healing intervene. When people have been abused or undernourished emotionally at home, they must acknowledge their parents' limitations and forgive their weaknesses. If they fail to do this, they are still bound.

Once a new family is formed, a couple must honor their parents, as the Fifth Commandment exhorts. But honoring parents does not require that we always obey them. Honoring parents means giving them the respect due to them, never renouncing the place they have in our lives. We cannot divorce our family but we can and must shift our primary loyalty from obeying parents to mutual submission to our marriage partner.

A person's childhood experiences, whether hurtful or not, can be the most significant asset one brings to the marital covenant, *if those experiences are properly understood.* There is no ideal family, but there is also no better place to learn how to make and keep a covenant than the family one is in.

It was crucial for Gail to learn how I related to my family. She saw me when I was angry with my parents, or just plain frustrated. She discovered that in spite of my struggling with their demands, I wanted to honor my parents. My mother was an especially hospitable person and loved to have people around. That has shaped my expectations for our home. Gail discovered the special relationship I have with my brother and has been able to support that over the years. And I made similar discoveries about the way Gail relates to her siblings and parents.

As unpopular as this concept might be, I believe a person's relationship to his parents is a partial indication of how he will relate to his spouse. Homely wisdom passed on in a psychologically unsophisticated culture went like this: "If you want to see how he will treat you in a few years, look at how he treats his mother. Look at how she relates to her father." This is oversimplified, but even this homespun wisdom is better than the modern delusion that one can start a new family and leave the old behind simply by getting married. We marry into a family. Indeed, we marry a family.

A SHORT EXERCISE

Here are some questions to answer by yourself, and then to share with your future marriage partner.

◆ When I was growing up, how did my family communicate feelings?
◆ How did my family understand the roles of husband and wife?
◆ How did my family solve conflicts?
◆ Were the members of my family able to say, "I love you"? If so, how? If not, why not?
◆ When I was younger, how did my parents show their love for me?
◆ Were the members of my family close? Did they feel supported and understood? Did some members feel the family was oppressively close, driving them to put distance between themselves and the rest of the family?
◆ Did I learn loyalty skills, namely how to assume responsibility for the well-being of family members in the face of outside threats?
◆ What values did I learn from my family?

◆How might I find it difficult to transfer my primary loyalty from my family of origin to my new family unit?

◆What elements of my family life would I most like to be incorporated into my new family unit?

◆What things about family relationships that I learned at home must be changed for me to have a successful marriage? What help will I need from my future partner, or from others, to make these changes?

10

Companionship Marriage

A college roommate of mine listed all the qualities he required in the woman he would marry. She was to be Miss Perfect. When he did finally marry, years later, I was dying to find out whether he had compromised—or whether, instead, *he* had developed the qualities he would need to be Miss Perfect's husband!

In this chapter and the next we will consider how a couple *cleaves*, or becomes united, to each other. We will do this from the perspective of what we can *give* to the relationship, not what we can get. And we will discuss *companionship*, a relatively modern expectation for marriage.

My mother came from a fishing village on the west coast of Newfoundland. Her father owned a sailing schooner and made two trips a year to Labrador, from which he would return after three months with the ship's hold groaning with a catch of salt cod. When he was not at sea, he was in the woods cutting timber. He did stay home long enough, however, to conceive twelve children and to communicate his love to each of them.

But marriage was different then. My grandparents married for survival. They hoped they would bring living children into this world and be able to harvest enough fish and grow enough potatoes to feed them. The concept of personal fulfillment was jibberish.

But in the Western world, according to Dr. William Glasser of reality therapy fame, we have moved from a survival culture to an identity culture.[1] We do not seek to marry a coworker in the task of survival with whom we procreate children and who will care for us when we are old. We marry to have a companion in the search for our own identity. In our modern society, survival depends on discovering and realizing our personal identities. We think that our marriage partner must help us do this.

I agree with David Mace, a marriage enrichment expert, that there are some basic changes taking place in marriage and family today:

- ◆ Marriage has changed from an institution to a companionship arrangement.
- ◆ Marriage has moved from partners with fixed roles to partners with fluid roles.
- ◆ The extended family has been supplanted by the nuclear family.
- ◆ Marriage has moved from being procreative-centered to being unitive-centered (centered on creating and enjoying unity).
- ◆ Marriage has changed from a short-span institution to a long-span institution (people live longer!).
- ◆ The family has moved from the one-vote system (father calls the shots) to the two-vote system.
- ◆ We have moved from an in-group type of marriage to an out-group type of marriage (from

marriage within a closed social circle to marriage with a person in another social group).

◆ We are recovering in our time a more biblical view of sex, that is, one that is more positive.[2]

So not only in the area of sexuality but also in our search for companionship we are returning to a more biblical view. God said it was not good for Adam to be alone (Genesis 2:18). The first reason to get married then, according to God's design, was not to have a coworker but a companion. Being ready for companionship is another matter.

NOTES
1. Dr. William Glasser, speaking a few years ago at the University of British Columbia, Vancouver, B.C.
2. Adapted from David Mace, as quoted in Paul G. Hansen, "Family Relations and the Behavioral Sciences," in Oscar E. Feucht, ed., *Family Relationships and the Church* (St. Louis: Concordia Publishing House, 1970), page 177.

11

Right for Each Other

The emphasis of the Bible is not on finding the perfect companion, but on being a marriageable person yourself. So as we explore the personal part of the marriage triangle, we must ask what kind of lover we are.

The prophet Hosea speaks to the question of *becoming* the right person for marriage, not *finding* the right person. Hosea was speaking for God, while God courted His reluctant bride, Israel. Simultaneously, God was speaking not only *through* Hosea but *to* him as the prophet contemplated courting again his own reluctant bride: "I will betroth you to me forever; I will betroth you in righteousness and justice, in love and compassion. I will betroth you in faithfulness, and you will acknowledge the LORD" (2:19-20).

The Lord described five qualities of a loving person, and we can see how each is essential to the marriage covenant:

◆ *Righteousness*—the dignity of the covenant.
◆ *Justice*—the social implications of the covenant.

◆ *Steadfast love*—the glue of the covenant.
◆ *Mercy*—the passion of the covenant.
◆ *Faithfulness*—the amen of the covenant.

We will examine these qualities one by one in this chapter and the next.

RIGHTEOUSNESS: THE DIGNITY
OF THE COVENANT

The Hebrew word *sedek* means "right standing with God" that comes as a gift (Isaiah 59:17). Righteousness is that splendid innocence credited to people who cling to Jesus and what He did for them. The Apostle Paul spoke of this as being "justified by . . . faith" (Galatians 2:16). It is the state of being accepted and welcomed by a just God who justifies us through the Person and work of His Son, Jesus.

But *righteousness* also means having "right" relationships. The righteous person wants to do what is right, to care about justice, to care for the poor and oppressed. Righteousness involves taking care of our covenant relationships with God and significant others. In light of this, consider these questions:

◆ Do I know that I am in right standing with God through Christ? Do I know this with such assurance that I will not have to keep proving this by my performance?
◆ Do I want to submit every area of my life to God (money, vocation, ambition, sexuality)?
◆ Do I want to do the right thing, not the easy thing, with my life in the world?
◆ Is there any person with whom some act of

reconciliation is needed before I am free to make a righteous covenant in marriage?

JUSTICE: THE SOCIAL IMPLICATION OF THE COVENANT

Justice (Hebrew *misphat*) is the quality of being fair in our dealings with others. For example, Joseph, the foster-father of Jesus, was said to be a just man. When he learned of Mary's pregnancy "and did not want to expose her to public disgrace, he had in mind to divorce her quietly" (Matthew 1:19). He thought her pregnancy meant she belonged to someone else. Old Testament law provided for the stoning to death of an unfaithful fiancée (Deuteronomy 22:13-21). But Joseph's concern was to do the right thing. He thought he would divorce her privately and not bring her to open shame.

Later, when an angel of the Lord told Joseph in a dream to take Mary as his wife, bearing with her the public shame of a humanly inexplicable pregnancy, Joseph, the just man, once again did what was right. He had not wanted to betray God's standards, but he did want to obey God. Justice is the covenant worked out in just social relationships.

Long before we get into serious relationship, we must decide to treat those we date justly. For instance, convictions concerning physical affection must be settled ahead of time. When we are swamped by emotion in an intimate situation, it is hard to remember what the Bible says on the matter, or even what is right and loving.

Strong convictions are also necessary when deciding whom to date. One's will power can be eroded when a believer in Jesus becomes emotionally or sexually involved with an unbeliever. The Bible speaks clearly

and definitely of the unsuitability of such a union
(2 Corinthians 6:14-15), and married couples in this situation can confirm that their unequal spiritual orientation
brings pain to both partners. But a commitment to justice
ahead of time will keep you from this mistake.

With regard to justice, consider these questions:

- ◆ Will I resolve to be just toward the person I love,
  determining always to do what is right and best
  for him or her?
- ◆ If I have "gone too far" in physical affection,
  will I do the right thing by refusing to carry
  on this way, deciding to set firm limits to our
  physical affection until I am willing and able to
  make a complete marriage covenant? (Having
  intercourse outside the covenant is like steal-
  ing the blessings of the covenant without the
  responsibility.)

12

True to Each Other

There are certain qualities necessary for making a person marriageable. Let's take a look at three elements that are vitally important for staying true to each other.

STEADFAST LOVE: THE GLUE OF THE COVENANT

The Hebrew language has a special word for love within the covenant: *hesed*. This almost untranslatable word is rendered "lovingkindness," "steadfast love," "unfailing love," or just "love." But it is more than love. It is love plus loyalty.

God expresses *hesed* by refusing ever to divorce His people. He shows loyal affection to the people of His promise. He not only refuses to be unfaithful but also works to bless His covenant partners.

A woman exclaimed, "I am determined to stay in this wretched relationship until the day I die!" She thought she was keeping the marriage covenant because she had put divorce out of her mind. But she was actually breaking the covenant because she refused to bless her covenant partner. Covenant love is both loyal and affectionate. Are you capable of this?

Consider these questions:

◆ When I think about marriage, can I imagine any reasons for leaving my spouse rather than staying and solving our problems?

◆ Am I willing and able to be loyal to my partner even when I do not feel loving?

◆ Do I have a record of solving problems within relationships, or have I left a string of burned-out relationships behind me?

MERCY: THE PASSION OF THE COVENANT

Mercy is compassion. The Hebrew word *racham* combines the idea of a mother's love and a father's love and is used to describe God as a merciful parent (Psalm 145:8, Isaiah 49:15, Lamentations 3:22). The word speaks of kinship concern. "He's no burden," said the boy carrying another boy on his back. "That's my wee brother!"

Mercy means "feeling with" one's covenant partner. Today we talk a lot about empathetic listening. Empathetic listening doesn't mean one always agrees with one's spouse, but maintaining a cold computer-like rationality is not a show of mercy. The compassionate listener can say, "I feel. . . ."

When we listen mercifully we refrain from giving an immediate response (giving ourselves the opportunity to listen more); we affirm the other person's feelings; we identify those feelings ("Am I right that you are feeling frustrated?"); we stay on center, sticking with the topic until there is resolution. To show *racham* we stop what we are doing and give our full attention, looking into our friend's eyes. When mercy cannot be conveyed through words, sometimes simply giving a hug will do.

Listening is one way to show mercy. Another way is by showing forgiveness.

Often in the hurly burly of life, husbands and wives opt for a shallow relationship, downplaying the need for forgiveness. "Oh forget it. I'm not perfect either" or "That's just the way I am," are ways of evading the confession of sin and the healing of forgiveness. You can forgive another only when you acknowledge and accept the pain that has been inflicted upon you. Condoning or covering up the wrongdoing does not heal the pain it caused. Such silence is relational violence.

Once you have acknowledged the pain and hurt, you can turn it over to Jesus who suffered triumphantly on the cross for us. If we refuse to do this we might begin to cherish and nourish the pain. Better to let Him bear it.

Even if conflict or pain in our relationship is not our fault, we have a responsibility to seek out our spouse and put matters right. Healing comes in marriage when we can say, "I was wrong. I am sorry. Please forgive me."

Unforgiven hurt leads to anger, and anger turns to vengeance, depression, and bitterness. That is why Jesus gives no plan other than forgiveness for dealing with relational hurt. If forgiveness is not sought and given there is spiritual and emotional death, and a covenant without mercy.

Give some thought to the following:

◆ Am I becoming a person with the capacity to enter into someone else's predicament and feel with him or her?
◆ Am I disposed to be merciful, or do I normally

express judgment when I discover faults in others?

◆ What do I do when I am afraid that confessing my sin (and asking for forgiveness) may do more harm to my relationship than keeping it hidden?

◆ Am I ready to forgive my friend anything and everything?

FAITHFULNESS: THE AMEN OF THE COVENANT

Faithfulness is the quality of being unconditionally committed and utterly dependable. The Hebrew word *emuna* suggests firmness. It leads us to say, "You can count on me. God is totally dependable, and in Christ I too am becoming dependable." The English word *amen* comes from this Hebrew word. Therefore faithfulness is saying "amen," or "let it be," to the covenant.

Consider these questions as you assess your ability to be faithful:

◆ Am I dependable in keeping my word, in keeping appointments, in keeping promises?

◆ Am I a supportive person?

◆ Am I consistent? Is there any major dichotomy between my words and deeds, my inner life and my outer life?

We need all these qualities to become a good covenant partner: righteousness, justice, steadfast love, mercy, and faithfulness. No one has all those attributes, but you can confess your weaknesses to God and to your intended covenant partner and pray for grace to change.

In an outrageous cartoon, one middle-aged obese woman says to her obese husband, "If you had really loved me, you would have married someone else!" Sometimes true love will lead you to conclude that you, not your partner, are unsuited for marriage at this time. When such a decision springs from honest self-appraisal and not from self-hatred or a poor self-image, you are better off to postpone marriage indefinitely. Better to break up now than to break down later. Sometimes, if we love people we will *not* marry them. If we love ourselves, we will not marry an unsuitable person out of fear that we will always be alone.

13

Going All the Way

S exual readiness for the "one flesh" part of the marriage triangle is a difficult thing to grasp. Part of the reason is that people today think they are the most sexually sophisticated and experienced generation to have walked across the stage of history. Many people, indeed most, have gone "all the way" before marriage. In spite of this, perhaps because of this, we may never have had a more sexually insecure generation than this one!

A book I picked up entitled *When to Dump Your Date* shows how confused is our secular culture. The author reflects,

> How easy it used to be when the first night together was the wedding night, when two people embarked on those awkwardly intimate first moments already convinced that they were sure of each other . . . or at least after convincing themselves that they were convinced they were sure of each other. Nowadays, instead of First Night being graduation day for boy and girl who have become husband and wife, the

First Night is the College Boards (multiple choice
on birth control, true or false on performance,
fill-in-the-blank on infections) that determines
whether there will be a Second Night. . . . Maybe
these times are more liberated, but there is still the
need to be special, to feel you're the only one—a
feeling that is hard to summon up when that First
Night partner steps into the apartment with you
and makes a beeline for the telephone answering
machine. And then listens with the earplug.[1]

By defining Christian marriage as a covenant with
all three components present (leaving—wedlock, cleaving—companionship, and one-flesh consummation), we
know when God regards two people as actually married.
Intercourse does not define marriage, but it communi-
cates a marriage-like commitment. It was designed by
God to consummate the covenant, to make it definite.
There is no such thing as casual or recreational sex.

The Apostle Paul seems to be driving at this in
1 Corinthians 6:16 when he quotes our foundational Genesis text. Two people are joining themselves together in
a way that means marriage. They are so marked by that
union that they can never look each other in the eyes as
though they had not gone all the way. When Paul says all
other sins are "outside the body," he does not think of the
body as the physical shell of the person, but as the physical expression of the whole person. "He who sins sexually
sins against his own body [person]" (1 Corinthians 6:18).

There is forgiveness after such an act, and there
is healing. But a marriage-like encounter has occurred.
In a mysterious, even spiritual, way two people have
belonged to each other. Their persons have been affected
by the union.

If they choose to marry, they should not do so only because they have had intercourse. But if they do marry, they should admit that they deceived themselves into thinking they could separate sexual intercourse from marriage. The problem today with sex is not that we have under-sexed marriage but that we have under-married sex.

Many couples today have experienced several physically intimate relationships before they attempt to bond with one partner for life. They are like young people who have grown up in several foster homes, belonging partially to many, but belonging ultimately and finally to no one. Often without realizing it, people who experiment with premarital intercourse are eroding their capacity to keep the marriage covenant.

What is particularly tragic is that couples who live together before marriage think they are better prepared sexually for the time when they will legalize their relationship, but in fact they may have made marriage harder. A cartoon pictures two people talking after a wedding. "How was the wedding?" one asks. The other replies, "I can't get used to these modern ceremonies. Now instead of saying 'I do' they say, 'I already did.'"

It is estimated by the United States Bureau of the Census that if the number of people living together before marriage increases at the current rate, unmarried couples living together in the United States and Canada may outnumber married young couples.[2] No matter how common it becomes, premarital sex is not good marriage preparation. Some studies have also shown how destructive premarital sex can be.

Premarital sexual attitudes and behavior do not change when one marries. If one is willing to experience the sexual act outside the covenant before marriage, a higher level of probability exists that one will do the same afterwards.[3] Premarital sex discourages communication, making it difficult to deal with the thorny issues that must be talked about and worked through before marriage.

Speaking to this problem Dr. Walter R. Schumm, a researcher of sexual behavior, says, "Once an imbalance develops between emotional intimacy and physical intimacy, the effect can spiral in an escalating fashion as more and more sex is needed to offset growing doubts about the underlying strength of the relationship."[4] Schumm suggests that for positive, not merely negative, reasons couples should reserve intercourse for marriage. A couple can then say, "This is something unique in space and time to our relationship alone. No one else has or will ever share it. It is something of ourselves and for ourselves that is very, very special, for us alone to cherish and enjoy."[5]

Contrary to the lie promoted by our hedonistic society, maximum sex is not kinky sex but covenant sex. Where there is public belonging and many other expressions and languages of love—in a word, where there is a divorceless covenant—there is opportunity for maximum sex. For sex to mean all it might, there needs to be a psychological intimacy to match the physical. Christians have the added gift of shared communion with God. Sex is not simply something you do. It is who you are. You can't "make" love. You just love.

The first act of such self-giving requires both a knowledge of who you are and a secure relationship in which such intimacy can be safely risked. For some couples it is already too late to save this for marriage. But it is not too late to seek forgiveness, healing, and to prepare oneself rightly for marriage now.

NOTES
1. Lois Romano, *When to Dump Your Date* (New York: Ballantine Books, 1984), page 15.
2. Quoted in Dennis B. Guernsey, *A New Design For Family Ministry* (Elgin, Ill.: David C. Cook, 1982), page 57.
3. L. H. Bukstel, G. D. Roder, P. R. Kilmann, J. Laughlin, and W. M. Sotile, "Projected Extramarital Sexual Involvement in Unmarried College Students," *Journal of Marriage and the Family* (1978), volume 40, pages 337-340.
4. Walter R. Schumm and George A. Rekers, "Sex Should Occur Only Within Marriage" (unpublished manuscript, Kansas State University, 1984), page 10.
5. Schumm, page 13.

14

The Celebration of Sex

Often people are surprised to learn that the Bible is explicit on the subject of sex. It shows us that sex powerfully seals the marriage covenant. One of the Bible's favorite words to describe the sexual encounter is *know*. It means to relate mentally, emotionally, spiritually, and physically to another person. This kind of knowing brings spice and depth to a marriage.

God is interested in people-making. He made us male and female and called us to be fruitful (Genesis 1:28). That is one of the blessings of sexuality. But God has a bigger view of sexual intercourse than its role in making babies. It is a language of companionship. It is an adult way to play. It is a physical way to communicate an emotional and spiritual reality. It is marital communion.

Marriage and family author Dolores Leckey says that because sex is so earthy, so sweaty, so downright human, it is an act of personal covenant: "It is the extension and fulfillment of the partners' ministry to each other begun during the public statement of vows." She further suggests that just as the spiritual reveals the physical, so the physical reveals the spiritual. Sexual intimacy is a double knowing, knowing the beloved other, but also knowing ourselves. Just as bread and wine are used in communion to deepen our love for God, so in marriage our bodies can be used to express something deeply personal and spiritual.[1]

One whole book of the Bible, the Song of Songs, is devoted to the celebration of erotic love within a covenant of reverence and loyalty. By giving us an example of two people celebrating sex, rather than by writing a manual on how to have sex, the biblical author motivates and inspires, rather than instructs and teaches. It provides our imaginations with images that are healthy and wholesome and awakens in us thanksgiving for God's good gift.

Our society tells us that sex is a skill to be learned and if not learned well before marriage could cause disaster. In contrast, the Bible shows us that the fullness of sexual expression cannot be "tried" because marriage cannot be tried. This means that two people who are sexually naive and inexperienced are at a distinct *advantage* when they marry. They have the privilege of expressing their embodying love and sexuality within the uniqueness and privacy of their own unrepeatable relationship. Instead of being sexually insecure, they are sexually empowered by the biblical vision of complete sexual union within the covenant.

In my opinion, there are too many books on sexual technique. It might be a good thing to ignore them and to let your marriage partner, not some world-renowned psychologist, become the expert on how he or she wishes to be loved. No one can tell you how to love your spouse better than your spouse. If your spouse says, "I am satisfied," then you have loved successfully, no matter what the various experts say in their books.

The Song of Songs shows two people experiencing the right kind of infatuation, courting each other within their marriage. It reveals two lovers preparing each other to experience the pleasure of lovemaking and wisely warning each other not to be aroused prematurely (2:7). It shows us two lovers admiring details about each other in a way that would be embarrassing if overheard by anyone else (4:10). It shows us two people reveling in the exclusiveness (5:1) and privacy of their lovemaking, with God the only rightful observer. Some commentators believe that it is God who utters these encouraging words in the Song: "Eat, O friends, and drink; drink your fill, O lovers" (5:1).

By showing us a healthy God-inspired and God-pleasing sex, the Bible invites us to repent from lust and to learn to love well. Not only should we repent of the filth and emptiness of our sex-gone-wrong society, but we should embrace sexual health as proclaimed in the Bible. God's gift of sex is a further illustration of the principle given by the Apostle Paul that "God's kindness [in this case His perfect plan] leads you toward repentance" (Romans 2:4).

NOTE
1. Dolores Leckey, *The Ordinary Way: A Family Spirituality* (New York: Crossroad, 1982), page 17.

15

Sexual Readiness

Some couples find it hard to imagine that the question of when and how to have a sexual encounter could ever be a problem within marriage. Surely any old time and way would be just fine—and the more often the better. But in fact good communication about sexual matters is not as simple as saying, "Let's make love tonight." The reason is that intercourse is not something you do so much as it is an expression of your whole marriage relationship.

Therefore, one of the most delicate things in marriage is the matter of saying, "Yes, I'd like to," or "Frankly, I'm super-tired tonight, and I would prefer to get a good night's sleep so I can be a better lover tomorrow. Is that all right?" For one partner to ask, "Do you want to make love?" is a trap, because it puts all the initiative on the responder to the question.

Many married couples resort solely to nonverbal signals—a light left on, a special nightie, a favorite fragrance, an evening shower, or a lit candle. These signals are just fine, as long as the signals given and received are clear to both. But there is nothing better than talking openly before, during, and after a sexual experience.

Talking about sex—your expectations, desires, and even your worries—is vitally important before marriage. But is it important to do more than talk? Is a growing physical experience before your wedding day a good way of preparing yourself for marriage?

The Bible gives no clear-cut answers to these questions. If it did, it might not fit each unique couple. And it might relieve you of the challenge of becoming a mature person with self-control, love, patience, and faith. According to the Bible, a person who lives by rules (even good ones) can be as self-centered as one who rejects all rules and lives for pleasure. Neither the legalist nor the licentious person pleases God (Romans 2, Galatians 2:15-16), a fact that is as controversial today as it was in the first century. So both those who insist that people conform to strict rules in premarital behavior and those who insist there should be none have missed the main purpose of the Christian faith: to make people fully human and mature as they progressively respond to the love of Christ.

What we are given in the Bible is something far more useful than a detailed description of permissible and forbidden behaviors. We are given an empowering vision of the goal of our marital preparation. Envisioning marriage as a lifelong covenant between two persons means that sex would be perverted if reduced to a mere physical activity. It is the sacrament of marriage. God says it is good. After all, He invented it.

God not only offers us a vision but also empowers us to live by that vision. He is willing to equip us to wait for marriage to express ourselves sexually and to fulfill the marriage covenant with love rather than lust (Hebrews 13:4). As we walk in the Spirit and nurture the fruit of the Spirit (love, joy, peace, patience, kindness, goodness, faithfulness, gentleness and self-control), we are liberated from catering to mere impulse and to what human nature has become through sin (Galatians 5:16-26). Psychologists tell us that impulse control is a vital step in maturity and marital readiness. In fact we do not love until we can control our impulses. "Love . . . is not rude [sexually or any other way], it is not self-seeking" (1 Corinthians 13:5). Love does not ask, "How far can I go before I am married?" but "How can I best respect the integrity and purity of my future partner?"

Lewis Smedes has given us three helpful principles of healthy sexual expression, which I will reframe in my own words:

- ◆ It is an expression from and to a *person*, not merely a body, and a measure of the relational commitment. Therefore one must never "say" something sexually that one is not saying at all other levels within the relationship.
- ◆ It is an expression of God's celebration of the complementarity between the sexes. That is, male and female differences are to be celebrated. Sex as God intended is heterosexual and exalts the other's otherness.
- ◆ It is an expression of a committed relationship and directed toward consummation within the covenant of marriage.[1]

Within this framework, is it wise to express ourselves physically in a progressive, controlled, and appropriate way before the vows are taken? Following are some thoughts distilled from experience (my own and others) and from my pondering God's plan for our sexuality.

Personally, I am not prepared to let our sick society destroy something beautiful that God has made, that is, a loving, responsible, and progressive expression of affection through which couples may prepare in a natural way for marriage. The view of an ancient wise man in Scripture is one of humble reverence, not dark fear: "There are . . . things that are too amazing for me . . . the way of a man with a maiden" (Proverbs 30:19).

First, there is no situation where premarital foreplay and intercourse are right for a couple because there is not a corresponding public and private covenant. Sexual foreplay and intercourse are covenant disciplines and covenant delights. Couples who are petting to mutual orgasm or engaging in oral sex can hardly think they are entering marriage as virgins. Scripture refers to this as "defrauding" each other (1 Thessalonians 4:6). True love is always willing to wait.

Second, physical affection should always lag behind a couple's level of commitment, because it is all too easy for physical closeness to take priority in the relationship. Until you are married, you are not married. Since an engagement may be broken, it is unwise (and unkind) to engage in any act that one would later regret if your friend were to marry someone else.

Third, foreplay (touching and stimulating the genitals) is exactly what the term implies: a playful preparation for intercourse. Foreplay prepares the body for intercourse in a number of physiological ways. Bringing each other to this "point of almost no return" before marriage is setting each other up for frustration or a stolen covenant.

Fourth, couples should read and discuss Scripture passages on love, lust, sex inside marriage, and sex outside marriage (for example, 1 Corinthians 6:12–7:40;

Ephesians 5:3,22-23; 1 Thessalonians 4:3-8; Hebrews 13:4). They should also pray together about their physical relationship. Certainly, they should discuss together what is appropriate sexual behavior in their relationship.

Fifth, since I am proposing the value of a long friendship prior to engagement, couples will need to learn to be satisfied with very simple forms of affection—hugging and kissing—for a long time. Many Christian leaders teach that there should be *no* physical affection until engagement, and only kissing and warm hugging between the engagement and the marriage. Although I believe this might be wise counsel sometimes, I cannot recommend this as a rule for everybody. Certainly one is hard pressed to defend this as an explicit biblical requirement. Usually the argument for no physical expression of affection is based on the assumption that one enters something like a hypnotic state during such displays of love in which complete control of oneself is lost. In fact, we are always able to be in control of ourselves and to know what we are doing.

Sixth, expressing affection in simple and appropriate ways is one of the processes of learning about each other and ourselves. Where there is self-control and love, this affection can be pleasing to God. Gail and I were drawn to each other physically, as well as in other ways, and this was important to us. Our mutual physical attraction was one of several signals that we were right for each other. If it had been the main signal, then we would be making too much of it.

NOTE
1. Adapted from Lewis Smedes, *Sex For Christians* (Grand Rapids, Mich.: Eerdmans, 1976), page 42.

16

Sexual Hurt

Sometimes painful revelations occur during the period of premarital sexual preparation. When one partner feels all physical affection is shameful and dirty, something will have to change or the marriage will probably be a sexual desert. It is better to get counseling for this kind of problem before marriage rather than after the ceremony.

In the case where one person has already had sexual intercourse with someone else, it is essential that this be revealed at an appropriate stage of the premarital relationship. Details of place, name, time, and events are not only unnecessary but unwise. When the virgin partner, even with the help of a counselor, cannot accept the nonvirgin partner as he or she is, the two should not marry. Failure to deal with this impasse may drag sexual guilt into marriage, with the sexually active person before marriage becoming the sexually frozen person after marriage. The same pattern of mutual disclosure is important for any homosexual encounter or a habitual masturbation problem.

One in four women have been sexually abused, some by a father or brother. They may bring into marriage fears that they will never enjoy the sexual experience after they are married. "Trying" intercourse with their future partner to make sure they can "do it" may seem to dispel the fear, but it will never heal the wounds. When, after marriage, the husband initiates sex in ways similar to his wife's abuser, her mind will play the old message of hateful fascination—partly loving it and partly hating it.

Much simpler, nonsexual forms of affection over a long period of time are a better indication than having intercourse of whether a person freezes at the touch of the opposite sex or is genuinely responsive. Counseling to help resolve the effects of rape, incest, sexual abuse, and abortion are advised before marriage rather than after. But better after than not at all.

In a healthy relationship where love is expressed physically, a person can learn respect for another's responsiveness, needs, limits, and hurts. Good verbal feedback patterns can be learned before marriage.

It would be gravely irresponsible to fail to address young adults today with a sexual morality that is both workable and thoroughly Christian. It is one of the many areas where the church should be a pioneer, and not merely the ambulance for this sick society.

A SHORT EXERCISE

◆ I see sexuality as a gift from God in this way . . .
◆ What I find hardest to believe about sex as a gift from God is . . .
◆ The most important thing my future spouse needs to know about my attitude toward sexual intercourse is . . .

◆My parents' model and teaching in sexual matters was an influence on me positively in this way . . . and/or negatively in this way . . .

◆The greatest fear I have in approaching the sexual part of our future relationship is . . .

◆What my future spouse needs to know about me in order for me to be sexually responsive is . . .

◆I think the initiative for having a sexual experience should come from . . .

◆The best way for us to communicate our desire for physical affection is . . .

◆I think we should be able to talk about sexual temptations we are having outside of our relationship, because . . .

◆One thing we must talk about before we marry concerning my past is . . .

17

Power and Partnership

G ail and I think we have a fairly "liberated" Christian marriage. When we answer questionnaires about how we make decisions when buying things, making love, or going on a vacation, we discover that we are equally involved. Once after rediscovering such egalitarian togetherness, I asked Gail, "If we are equal partners, then how can I be your 'head' as the Bible says in Ephesians 5:23?"

"Quit complaining," she said. "That is why it is so easy for me to let you be the head." That spontaneous answer holds the key to biblical headship and submission.

The issue of power is a very important matter when married. Every marriage is either a one-vote or a two-vote affair. It is important to unite together on your votes, or else be willing to give in, when appropriate, to your spouse. It is far better to discuss each other's agenda for power before getting married than after.

Occasionally a man exercises control in a marriage in the form of raw executive power, sometimes labeled as biblical headship. He makes decisions overtly or secretly for his wife. Both partners can control each other by using anger, or withdrawing affection, money, or other essentials. Sometimes wives try to take control of the relationship by playing the victim, by crying "poor me," by being constantly sick, or by refusing to make decisions.

Husbands who on the surface may seem to be weak and spineless may very well control the relationship, sometimes without realizing it, by refusing to take charge of their own lives, thus forcing their wives to assume control. It is widely recognized that the person least interested in the relationship is the most powerful. He calls the shots by appearing to be indecisive.

Usually such power-plays surface long before a couple gets to the altar. The less interested person distances himself (or herself) from his partner, forcing her to pursue. If the pursuer stops chasing, the distancer usually stops running. This sad game of hide-and-seek is played by many couples before marriage, and should certainly be stopped before it becomes institutionalized as a way of life in marriage.

One serious form of control that may surface during courtship involves the person who threatens suicide when his or her friend wants to break up. Any intimidation that makes ending the relationship seem morally impossible is a power play. Such behavior makes one person in the friendship feel trapped. And no one can be trapped into a covenant. Such a couple simply should not marry, at least not yet!

A covenant cannot be made without consent. This is something the Christian Church has always insisted on. And consent cannot be merely verbal, but must come from the *heart*. One young woman said that when the pastor in her wedding service asked if anyone could show any just cause why she and her future husband should not be lawfully married, she wanted to yell, "I have an objection!" She thought it was too late to back out, but it was not. It would have been better to turn around and leave the ceremony than to spend the next few years finding a legal way out of the marriage.

So, power is a big issue to resolve before your wedding day. The Christian approach to the politics of marriage calls for radical submission to one another. Mutual submission lifts husband and wife beyond control and compliance and enables them to yield rights to each other, harmonize personal interests, make decisions mutually, and empower each other. The husband empowers his wife by meeting her needs, respecting her limits, and sacrificing for her. The wife empowers her husband by honoring and respecting him. In both cases we are speaking about gifts and graces, not about duties and rights.

Unfortunately, the idea that the husband especially is supposed to wield power over the wife is presented by some people as "the biblical pattern." That kind of marital tyranny betrays a serious misunderstanding of Scripture.

In some ways Gail and I have a fairly traditional marriage. We think we have biblical reasons for not succumbing to the roleless, matched-career, androgynous partnership being marketed as marriage in secular society. The cry for "equal rights for equal persons" has made us lose something biblically precious: the husband-wife relationship as an analogy of Christ's relationship with His bride, the Church.

The biblical teaching from the Apostle Paul is simply that a husband should love his wife sacrificially as Jesus loved the Church and gave Himself up for her (Ephesians 5:25). The husband loves his wife more than she deserves;

that is his gift to her and that is what headship means for a man in marriage. All over the world those words are countercultural, especially where husbands think that headship means the wielding of power. The husband is not called to be a benevolent monarch in the home, but simply to be benevolent. He is empowered to be "head" in this way because Jesus is *his* head. The husband is not told to expect obedience or to make sure his wife is submissive. He has his own high calling from God as a uniquely appointed husband for his wife.

Similarly, when Paul speaks to wives, he does not tell them to make sure their husbands give them Christlike love and self-sacrifice. A wife has her own high calling, too. A wife gives the gift of headship to her husband in the currency of "submission" (Ephesians 5:22,24) and "respect" (5:33). That does not mean a wife is bound to do everything a husband says without a peep or a whimper. No man in his right mind wants his wife to be his subject, and even Christ does not treat His Church as a slave-servant but rather as a partner-friend (John 15:15, Ephesians 5:25).

A SHORT EXERCISE

The purpose of this exercise is to help you explore some of the husband/wife role-models you will bring to marriage. What is crucial is not that you accept someone else's description of husband-wife roles, but that you and your friend agree. I suggest you each answer the following questions separately and then compare your responses.

◆In your parents' marriage, how are the following decisions made? Put a P, for parents, where it fits best on the scale of 1-5:

	Wife 1	2	Fully Shared 3	4	Husband 5
Who makes large purchases.					
How the children are raised.					
How leisure time is spent.					
What the family does for spiritual education.					
When to see relatives.					
What to do for a vacation.					
Where to live.					
On social life and friendships.					
How money is saved and spent.					
When lovemaking happens (if known).					

◆ Now go through the list again and place an M in the column that best represents how you want those same decisions to be made in your marriage. Remember, do not share this with your future spouse until you have answered honestly. Then compare your answers and talk about the results.

◆ Do you think the roles of husband and wife should be different from that of your parents? How?

◆ What can your future spouse do to empower you and make you feel in charge of your own life?

◆ What does your future spouse need to know about you before you can function well as a husband or wife?

18

Headship Within Equality

For many people today the ideal marriage involves interchangeable roles. They want to eliminate such rich words as *husband* and *wife* and replace them simply with *spouse*. In face of the reckless trend in Western society toward androgyny (the merging of the sexes), I now wish to make a case for sexual differences in marriage, even though those differences are hard to define and even more difficult to encapsulate in marriage roles.

In general it seems that "feminine" characteristics, (such as intuition, emotional transparency, responsiveness, and relational empathy) and "masculine" characteristics (such as rationality, restrained emotionalism, and aggressiveness) are qualities found in both sexes and are culturally affected. There are, however, clusters of characteristics that normally are found more in one or the other sex. I admit that this subject is hotly debated.[1] But for centuries the evidence of a difference between masculine and feminine has been unquestioned, and we certainly have a scriptural reason to celebrate that difference. Marriage, as the Apostle Paul said, is "a profound mystery . . . about Christ and the church" (Ephesians 5:32). It is an earthly parable of a heavenly mystery. Living out the mystery at home means that marriage can be experienced on a deeper level when there is a husband and a wife, rather than just two "spouses" who have mutually interchangeable "roleless" roles.

I think it is fortunate that the Bible does not spell out detailed roles for men and women in marriage. Not a single verse gives a job description for the husband or the wife. Ephesians 5:21-33 describes the spirit, the shape, and the reason for mutual submission of husband and wife, but it does not define roles.

Being husband and wife is *not* like speaking and acting the parts in a drama according to a prepared script. It is more like writing our own play according to an outline written by someone else. We know how the play ends, what our parts are, and why we are playing those parts. The play ends with the great wedding of Christ (the Groom) and the Church (the bride). The plot line is the adventure of discovering that the nitty-gritty experiences of married life can become windows of the soul. We also know why we are playing the parts: it is an act of worship to Christ, or as Paul says, "out of reverence for Christ" (5:21).

Couples are free to write their own lines according to the personalities and gifts God gave them. No one can play someone else's role. As Patricia Gundry says in *Heirs Together*, "How can I love the real you when you are trying so hard to be someone else? And how can you love the real me when I am trying to be someone else?"[2]

Although I am unable to define in detail what it means for the husband to be head, I believe that something of substance can and should be said. Headship in marriage, as I understand it, is a priority within a relationship of equals. On the husband's part, this priority means that he is the first to be willing to go the way of the Cross, the first to sacrifice in the relationship. On the wife's part the priority involves giving the gift of honor and respect that places her husband first in the relationship. When husbands and wives relate to each other in those ways, they experience full partnership, equality, and complementarity.

I admit that it is hard to speak of "priority within a relationship of equals," but that is because we cannot think of many human societies where there is both genuine equality and priority within relationships. Marriage, however, is designed to be a mystery of God, and therefore we must look for a transcendent model.

The biblical mandate to live according to that model comes not only from Paul's direct statement in Ephesians 5:33 but also from the fact that male and female are made in the image of God (Genesis 1:27).

Headship involves honoring, nurturing, loving, and building the marriage relationship. It means that normally the man is responsible for providing for his wife and children and for protecting both the relationship and his wife.

In the "play" Gail and I are writing, it works out this way. We share as fully as possible the leadership of the marriage and home. But if the marriage begins to suffer or our love grows cold, I believe it is my responsibility to be the first to initiate steps toward the renewal of our marriage covenant. In practice most women are the first to be concerned about their marriage, and indeed Gail is often more sensitive to marital problems than I. So I see her input in this area as a great corrective for my oversights.

While both of us speak for our marriage and represent our home publicly, Gail defers to my representative leadership of the home in some situations when she would be just as capable of speaking for us. Other times I defer to her. She does not feel the buck stops with me even though I happen to keep our financial accounts. We try to make all decisions mutually. (In emergency situations one of us always takes over—but not always the same one!) When there is an impasse, we wait, work, and pray until we can both fully own the final decision. We find that the process of mutual decision making is more upbuilding to our faith and life together than simply deciding that one partner has more clout. Some couples work it out by putting the husband in charge and giving the wife veto power! But I think that approach is more open to abuse.

Providing physical protection seems to me to be an obvious headship responsibility, because usually the woman is physically weaker than the man. Even so, we must admit the superlative powers of women to endure physical suffering. When Gail and I are traveling in dangerous situations, I feel it is my job to protect her. Protection is not solely the husband's duty, though. In many ways Gail protects me, especially emotionally.

Every marriage has at least the potential of children, and Gail and I have had the privilege of enjoying three, all now married and away from home. Often, when the children are young, it is neither possible nor advisable for the mother to provide for her family, except in case of extreme emergency. Therefore, I have tried consistently to provide for Gail, but without preventing her from working outside the home. From time to time we have shared remunerative employment. Frankly, her work in the home, while not technically remunerated, has been more important than most of what I have done outside. It is vitally important to discuss work, income, children, and so on, before you are married.

I believe that as husband I am called to be the first to take leadership in the home, whether in planning, family Christian education, or childrearing. Often I do not do so, and so I am thankful when Gail takes leadership instead of goading and nagging me to be someone I am not or to do something I have no heart for.

Gail equips me to lead by prizing the leadership I do take. I am called to welcome and prize the initiatives she takes and the ideas she advances. Gail has graciously decided that the location of my out-of-the-home vocation will be our primary place of residence, but I have made the choice not to move from time to time even when a vocational advance was in the wind, because of Gail's work and ministry as well as the stability we desired for our children. In lovemaking I am usually the first to express interest, but I am delighted when Gail takes the initiative. By no means do I feel this is a threat to my being a husband or "head."

In fact, we rarely ever talk about my being head except when someone wants to know how such a role has worked out in our lives. But we are conscious from time to time of the mystery-play we are living out. And we find that the dynamic of our relationship brings us closer to God and evokes our faith. Increasingly we see that "husband" and "wife" are not so much roles to be performed as special people we are becoming as Christ lives in us and through us in our home.

So, that is what it is like for us. But if you have been thinking as you read these words that it will be different in your marriage, I want to affirm that it *should* be, for it is *your* marriage. So write your own parts!

The mystery of marriage is that there is unity because there is differentiation, and headship is one way we must speak about sexual differentiation in God's marriage design. No matter what happens in our society, Christians should continue to celebrate the difference between male and female, husband and wife. This is a profound mystery, Paul says in Ephesians 5:32, because it concerns Christ and the Church. Christ is the key to marital harmony, not some standardized male or female job description. Throughout the passage in Ephesians, Paul emphasizes that he is not interested primarily in female capitulation or even in mutual submission. His focus is Christ: "Submit to one another out of reverence for Christ" (5:21); "Wives, submit . . . as to the Lord" (5:22); "Husbands, love . . . as Christ" (5:25); and "I am talking about Christ and the church" (5:32).

Christ is the recipient of our daily marital ministry to our spouse. He is also the inspiration for it. That is the mystery that is cracked open each time we live the gospel out in our marriages, our homes, and our churches. Ephesians 5:21-33 does not describe the duties of Christian husbands and wives. It is a statement of marital spirituality. Loving, submitting to, and respecting your spouse are acts of worship.

C. S. Lewis uses the analogy of the bow and the string on a cello or violin. Both are needed to make one sound. There is more unity and beauty with a bow and a string than in a room full of bows, or a room full of strings.

Some people would rather not have any mystery. They want male and female roles put down in black and white. They want relationships arranged in neat hierarchies. They want the functions of the sexes institutionalized in job descriptions and sexually determined leadership offices. Others want to strip away the mystery by unisexing everything, including the mutual ministry of husband and wife.

For my part, I will devote myself to the lifelong—indeed, eternity-long—adventure of discovering the mystery. The unity of the sexes is nothing less than the mystery of Christ. Equipping our own marriages for full male-female partnership is itself an act of worship. As Lewis said so insightfully, we are "not as when stones lie side by side, but as when stones support and are supported in an arch. . . . Thus each is equally at the centre and none are there by being equals."[3]

NOTES

1. An example of this debate is found in the book edited by Carol Gilligan, *Mapping the Moral Domain* (Cambridge, Mass.: Harvard University Press, 1989) in which Gilligan reinterpreted Kohlberg's theory of moral hierarchy. Kohlberg maintains that boys grow through several stages of moral development ending on the level of making moral choices through abstract justice, while girls never get beyond the level of asking what moral choices do to relationships and what harm will come. That, Ms. Gilligan argues, may not be a sign of moral inferiority on the part of females, as is alleged by Freud, Piaget, and others, but a special moral superiority that females bring to the matters of justice.
2. Patricia Gundry, *Heirs Together: Mutual Submission in Marriage* (Grand Rapids, Mich.: Zondervan, 1980), page 137.
3. From C.S. Lewis, *Voyage to Venus: Perelandra* (London: Pan Books, 1963), pages 199, 201.

A SHORT EXERCISE

Read Ephesians 5:22-33, and then discuss the following questions:

◆ How will an understanding of headship help you sort out the roles you discussed at the end of the last chapter?

◆ Why is it better to do what fits your relationship and

works best for you rather than what others expect of you?

◆Which husband/wife roles presented by Christian teachers do you affirm? Cannot affirm?

◆What does it now mean to you to be a "husband" or a "wife"?

19

A Permanent Wedding Gift

You can give your intended spouse a wedding gift that costs nothing but time and can be given every day of your life together: *prayer*. Many couples today want to share a common spiritual pilgrimage. They have good reason. It is not only our bodies and minds that marry, but our spirits. For couples who want to love their Creator together the most important spiritual discipline of all is praying for each other. Praying *with* each other is a great thing but praying *for* each other is even greater. You can give this gift when you get up in the morning, when shaving, or blow-drying your hair, while driving to work or college, while relaxing in a comfortable chair or escaping to a retreat center for reflection and prayer. Let me explain why this gift is so valuable.

First, *praying is a way of getting help for the relationship.* When we pray for each other we cooperate with the ongoing intercession of the Holy Spirit. The Apostle Paul told the Romans that "the Spirit helps us in our weakness. We do not know what we ought to pray for, but the Spirit himself intercedes for us with groans that words cannot express" (Romans 8:26). When we reach out to touch our spouse emotionally and spiritually, we feel sometimes as if we are on a long journey. But praying for our spouse is like stepping on a moving sidewalk or an escalator. The Spirit is already praying for our loved one; we are merely joining in. Prayer is the most direct way of getting help for our marriage. Our therapist is always *in*!

Second, *prayer for each other gives us a new viewpoint*—the mind of Christ. Even during courtship it is easy to focus on our friend's faults and weaknesses. But as we pray "we regard no one from a worldly point of view" (2 Corinthians 5:16). We begin to look at him or her as God does, with strengths and potentials to be prized. We gain God's hope for our partner. Even if our friend is not changed, or seems not to be, *we* are changed in a crucial area, our personal attitude. We accept because we have been accepted. We love less conditionally because we have been loved by God unconditionally.

Third, *prayer for each other invigorates the relationship*. We discover that Christ is not only the glue of the marriage covenant but the joy of it. Without Him our marriage is like a soft drink with the fizz worn off, stale and tasteless. With Him, all of life, even the sweaty and hard parts, becomes worship. The famous marriage passage in Ephesians 5:21-33 is not primarily concerned about Christian behavior in marriage but about the relationship of marriage to Christ. Husbands are called to love *as* Christ loves (5:25). Wives are called to respect as to the Lord (5:22). Both are called to submit to each other as part of their ministry to Jesus (5:21). This is a spiral of intimacy. What we do to our spouse is what we do to Jesus, who sometimes comes to us as the least of our brothers and sisters in need (Matthew 25:35-36,40). The closer we get to Christ, the closer to each other; the closer to our spouse, the closer to Christ. Praying for each other is like oxygenating the relationship.

Fourth, *prayer for each other keeps the relationship clean*. We are compelled to keep short accounts, to seek forgiveness and to give it. In Matthew 5:23-24, Jesus said that if you are offering your gift at the altar "and there remember that your brother has something against you, leave your gift there in front of the altar. First go and be reconciled to your brother; then come and offer your gift." This remembrance of sin is inspired by being in the presence of God in prayer. But in turn, making things right brings us into deeper intimacy with God—another upward spiral of grace.

Fifth, *praying for each other brings good results*. In prayer God gives His creatures the incredible gift of limited casualty. God is moved and so are we. Something happens. God does not promise to do exactly what we ask on our schedule. But we can be sure that no one has ever prayed in the name of Jesus and had *nothing* happen! I confess I do not understand exactly *how* God answers prayer, but it goes something like this: Jesus is the Mediator not only between God and mankind but also between husband and wife, friend and friend, friend and enemy. The most direct way to our beloved is through Jesus, the Go-between. He is influenced by our prayers but "filters" them according to what is best and strategic at the moment. So the result is a symphony of wills with everyone being influenced but no one manipulated. Some things cannot happen to our spouse unless we do pray. God will make sure that no matter how we pray the result will be beneficial and not destructive.

Sixth, *prayer for each other meets the deepest need*. What we need most is not a changed spouse but a life filled with the goodness of God. Someone was asked, "If your

God is as good as you say and knows what you need before you ask Him, then why should you need to ask Him?" The answer given was breathtaking: "What if God knows that what you need most is Himself, and what if your asking is His best opportunity of giving you Himself?" We need God more than we need our spouse. Our spouse needs God more than he or she needs us. Our spouse needs us to need God more than we need our spouse. Our spouse's deep needs will be better met partly through us if our deep needs are first met by God. So you have six good reasons to pray for your beloved. Any one would be sufficient reason to give this gift every day of your marriage. It can start today.

A SHORT EXERCISE

Find a quiet place to pray alone. (Later pray anywhere.) Using Paul's prayer in Ephesians 3:14-21, you can pray for your future spouse in this way:

◆ Pray for *strength in the inner person.* "He may strengthen you with power through his Spirit in your inner being" (3:16).
◆ Pray for *authentic spiritual life,* a person-to-person relationship with God: "That Christ may dwell in your hearts through faith" (3:17).
◆ Pray for *a deeper experience of being loved by God*: "Being rooted and established in love, may have power . . . to grasp how wide and long and high and deep is the love of Christ" (3:17-18). You can pray about this in terms of relationships, attitudes, goals, vocation, and personal self-esteem.
◆ Pray for *an assurance of being loved that is deeper than mere head knowledge*: "And to know this love that surpasses knowledge" (3:19).

◆ Pray for *a continuous filling of the presence and power of God*: "That you may be filled to the measure of all the fullness of God" (3:19).

◆ Pray for *a meaningful relationship with all God's people* so that all of the above will be "together with all the saints" (3:18).

20

An Army of Two

My marriage has not been completely free of conflict, but Gail and I have enjoyed a remarkable degree of comfort and peace within our relationship. We consider this not so much an accomplishment as a precious gift. But sometimes I think we sense that gift so keenly because we experience more conflict *outside* our marriage than *inside*. Why fight each other when we have a common enemy?

Spiritual friends *must* fight—not each other, but what Apostle Paul calls "the principalities and powers" (Ephesians 6:10-20). If you are a couple in Christ, you are drafted into a cosmic conflict with society, culture, spiritual realms, and Satan himself. As an army of two, you must develop a living understanding of Ecclesiastes 4:12: "Though one may be overpowered, two can defend themselves. A cord of three strands is not quickly broken." A war is raging, and two soldiers on the same side fighting each other have been dangerously diverted. Unlike all other human wars, this battle with evil is good—good because it addresses fundamental problems in marriage.

SEDUCTIONS

We need the full armor of God (Ephesians 6:13) to fight this multi-front battle with evil. Christian couples are assaulted on every side and in every way. Perhaps the most subtle attacks are the seductions of sensualism, secularism, and relativism.

Sensualism results when satisfying our senses keeps us from thinking or praying. Ours is a body culture. The majority of advertisements on the bus, subway, or television are for the improvement of the body and its sensual experience: the body must be fed, perfumed, oiled, lubricated, covered, uncovered, trimmed, and titillated. A *healthy sensualism* is described in Scripture, as witnessed in the inspired love song of the Song of Songs. Christians thankfully say that sex is good but not a god. The delight in each other's body is holy precisely when the beloved is more than a body—a covenant partner and spiritual friend.

But detached from the shelter of the marriage covenant, sex becomes exotic and then demonic. It takes control over us and demands more and more. Even some so-called Christian marriage partners seek ever kinkier sexual thrills. But eroticism sought for its own sake is subject to the law of diminishing returns. The force of this cultural pressure to find the center of life in the genitals is almost insurmountable.

Or take the impact of *secularism*. Someone defined secularism as "this is all there is-ism." Secularism says that man can live without God. Few Christians would believe that statement, but many live as though God were dead, as practical atheists. Their marriages are like houses fully wired for electricity but with the main switch turned off. There is no daily, passionate dependence on the Lord.

If God withdrew His Holy Spirit from their homes, they would still go off to work, feather their nests, plan their vacations, keep up their round of activities, and continue to boast about their accomplishments. Secularism, and its companion *materialism*, drift into our marriages like a fog.

Relativism is the belief that absolutes are obsolete. Everything is relative. All love is conditional. There is a "what if" in every clause, including the marriage covenant, which is no longer "for better, for worse, so long as we both shall live," but "for better, for riches, for health, so long as we both love . . . unless it doesn't work out." Most couples presenting themselves for marriage in the church are not aware that they have a culturally influenced *emotional loophole* in their wedding vows. What they exchange are not binding vows but statements of intention. To be married for good today one must engage in spiritual warfare.

STRUCTURAL EVIL

Paul uses four precise terms or phrases in Ephesians 6:12 to describe the dimensions of conflict we experience. The first mentioned are *rulers* (*arches*). The original language refers not only to leaders but also to realms of worldly life that become tools for an evil being behind the scenes—Satan. *Rulers* include political rulers, cultural, corporate, and even religious leaders, represented today by most of the names that are written up in *Time* magazine. As leaders are often corrupt, so also are the laws, customs, institutions, and structures that regulate life within society. Paul refers also to *powers* (*exousias*), or human authorities that have power to make decisions over us. Those people often make us feel that we are not in control of our own lives. Next are the *powers of this dark world* (*kosmodrator*), powers that dominate—whether they intend to or not—the cultural, social, political, and religious world. There are also *spiritual forces of evil in the heavenly realms* (*pneumatika*), or the spiritual pollution of our real life here and now. Paul proclaims that our life here and now is infiltrated by alien forces, powers, and persons that seek to dominate us. We cannot escape entirely from this in the Church, and Christian marriage offers no hermetically sealed shelter.

In a late-night discussion with my theological students in Kenya, I was able to look at the spiritual battle with regard to marriage from a cross-cultural perspective. I was surprised by some of the questions.

"Walimu (this means *teacher*), how can you know whether your wife can have children unless you have a child before marriage? It's too late to find out after!"

I replied that biblical marriage is first for companionship and only secondly for procreation. "Can you not trust God for a full life together in Christ even though you might not have the blessing of children?" I asked.

"But Walimu, if you find you have only girls is it really wrong to take a second wife in order to have a son?"

Gail and I swallowed hard and asked, "Can you tell us from the Bible why males are more important than females? Are both not equally precious to God and to Christian parents?" We were dealing not merely with a social custom but also with marital institutions that had taken on an idolatrous life of their own, having been co-opted by Satan. I invited the students to examine their culture in the light of Scripture rather than the other way around. But I knew I would have to do the same myself.

In a few short minutes my thoughts left the "survival culture" of tribal Kenya where marriage is for work (which is performed largely by the wife) and the preservation of the family, and I was once again in the "identity culture" of North America, where marriage is for happiness, personal fulfillment, self-actualization, and finding oneself. I wondered whether the *good* institution of marriage has been even more tragically colonized by the Enemy in our world than in the world of my Kenyan friends. Finally I said, "In my country the pursuit of happiness and personal fulfillment has become an idol. In order to worship this idol we do the exact opposite of you: We have as few children as possible and destroy the ones we do not want." I found it hard to confess this, but I knew in a deeper way that to be married for good and for God in either country means a faith-battle, arm-wrestling the institution of marriage into biblical conformity.

THE ENEMY

In Africa, where I am writing this chapter, the church has mature experience in overcoming the demonic through the power of Christ. In my opinion we have more to learn about signs and wonders from Africa than from Anaheim and especially more to learn about dealing with Satan himself. Paul says that the Church—and this includes the micro-church of husband and wife—should "put on the full armor of God so that you can take your stand against the devil's schemes" (Ephesians 6:11). Two dangers arise when dealing with Satan in spiritual warfare: one is to take him too seriously, the other is not to take him seriously enough.

We take Satan too seriously when we give him too much attention and become preoccupied with his schemes. Satan, biblically understood, is a little person whose defeat was accomplished when God's Kingdom was inaugurated (Revelation 11:15). Satan's doom is certain. He is having his last fling on earth because he has been kicked out of Heaven (12:10-12). He is not omnipotent, not omniscient, and not omnipresent.

But we may also err in not taking Satan seriously enough. There is *less* demonic activity than some people think and *more* than others think! No couple in Christ can afford to ignore the reality of a formidable enemy to their marriage, an evil, sinister spiritual being with personal characteristics who is determined to wean us from dependence on God. Satan is the enemy of spiritual friendship because he knows the awesome power of unity in Christ. Since he is a master of charades, he will come to us not so much in what is obviously satanic but in a seemingly spiritual act—such as condemning a fellow sinner. He is called the accuser of the brethren (Revelation 12:10), and marriage partners may unwittingly be his accomplices by joining Satan in condemning a child of God, one's own spouse. But the most common entree for the Devil in a Christian marriage is simply the refusal to forgive: "Do not let the sun go down while you are still angry, and do not give the devil a foothold" (Ephesians 4:26-27). Failure to forgive quickly gives place to doubting the goodness of God (and one's spouse), and finally to a bitter spirit. Satan wants to split up God's family, and he is determined to split up Christian marriages. I painfully conclude that the widespread breakup of the marriages of Christian leaders in North America is part of a sinister plot from the dark side of the universe that we have unconsciously aided and abetted. May it be said of us that "we are not unaware of his schemes" (2 Corinthians 2:11).

DISARMING THE POWERS

Seductions, structural evil, the Enemy, death—we do have formidable foes. No wonder Paul says we are *not* hand-wrestling merely flesh and blood. But Paul tells us to put on the armor of God *not* because the battle is so severe that we might not win, but because *the battle has already been substantially won*. Radical evil calls for a radical solution. The axis of the whole world must be moved. The level needed to do this must have its fulcrum outside the world. That frail cross of Jesus is the lever that has moved the world. This is the strength through weakness that is "divine power to demolish strongholds" (2 Corinthians 10:4). Jesus' death not only saves us from the guilt of individual sin but disarms the powers of evil. The resurrection is proof positive that seductions, structural evil, Satan's wiles, and the last enemy, death, are vanquished. The "thrones or powers or rulers or authorities" (Colossians 1:16) created by Christ and colonized by Satan may now be recreated *for* Christ. This is the mission of the Church (Ephesians 3:10). It is a strange war indeed, because as soon as we conquer the enemy we completely rebuild the enemy's kingdom at our own expense according to new standards.

SOMETHING TO DO! ARMING AN ARMY OF TWO

For this all-out battle every engaged couple needs the proper armor. As you read Ephesians 6:13-18, put on each piece of armor consciously either through silent prayer or by praying aloud.

The *belt of truth* means utter honesty and integrity, or "speaking the truth in love" (Ephesians 4:15). This is the "underwear" Christians wear. For couples this means being real with each other. The *breastplate of righteousness* means both righteous living and justification by faith that gives us the imputed righteousness of Christ (2 Corinthians 5:21). Our feet must be *fitted with the readiness that comes from the gospel of peace.* Roman soldiers were successful partly because of their thickly studded shoes that enabled them to cover long distances. Our spiritual readiness is the "go" of the gospel, and every couple that engages in some outreach to unbelievers is not only strengthened but *protected.* Mission is spiritual armor. The *shield of faith* was an image suggested by the Roman soldier's oblong, leather-covered shield used as protection against the enemy's flaming missiles. Hearty trust in God is the Christian's antiballistic missile shield, a puncture-proof shield to deflect Satan's attacks. The *helmet of salvation* suggests full assurance of salvation, which protects our thought life, and *the sword of the Spirit* is the preached and spoken word of God. Armed in this way, there is nowhere in the universe so demonic that a Christian couple might not be called by God to serve there. We can storm the gates of hell together (Matthew 16:18).

Those pieces of Christian armor are merely different ways of "putting on" Christ through living prayer. With *Christ's integrity* we can tell the whole truth to each other. With *Christ's righteousness* our heart is protected. With *Christ's gospel* our feet will never be dangerously idle. With *faith in Christ* the Devil's attacks are diverted even without our knowing. With assurance of *salvation in Christ* our thought life is protected. And with the *word of Christ* in our hearts and on our lips the Enemy can but vainly try to protect himself.

21

Why Jesus Goes to Weddings

Because marriage is so earthy, so sweaty, so personal, it is a peculiar pathway to God. We have a God who comes to earth, takes on flesh, and slips into a human family. We have a God who loves to dwell in a covenant.

The call to mutual submission in marriage is an invitation to allow our stony hearts to be plowed and furrowed by God, but not in a magnificent sanctuary with choir and acolytes. Rather, this holy work is done over a breakfast table of cold cereal, while we struggle to stretch our limited funds to pay all the bills, and in the privacy of the bedroom, where we desire to say "I love you" in a special, confidential way.

To submit to our spouse we must welcome the mutual incarnation of our lives, becoming like our spouse, taking on us our spouse's burdens and weaknesses. Marital life is to be a kind of living death to self, a daily path of self-denial. But through working together in love, that "death" turns out to be a type of resurrection. This makes every wedding day Christmas, Good Friday, and Easter

Sunday all rolled in one. No wonder Jesus wants to be there.

Weddings figured largely in the life, ministry, and teaching of Jesus. As a child He must have followed the crowds to watch weddings in Nazareth where He grew up. The children would stand on the sidelines watching the people dance, feast, and celebrate. The next day they would re-enact the whole thing children's style.

We have hints of such child's play in Jesus' teaching when He said,

> "To what can I compare this generation? They are like children sitting in the marketplaces and calling out to others:
>
>> "'We played the flute for you [at a wedding],
>>   and you did not dance;
>> we sang a dirge,
>>   and you did not mourn.'
>
> For John came neither eating nor drinking, and they say, 'He has a demon.' The Son of Man came eating and drinking, and they say, 'Here is a glutton and a drunkard, a friend of tax collectors and "sinners."'" (Matthew 11:16-19)

"Let's play wedding," some of the kids would suggest, but the children they asked were not in the mood. "Who feels happy today?" (Jesus compared His coming to a wedding celebration, whereas being with old sobersides John was like going to a funeral.) Other kids said, "Let's play funeral." But no one wanted to do that either. So the kids of Nazareth could not get their act together. Nothing would please them all.

But Jesus did not merely "play" wedding. He went to weddings. Jesus worked His first miracle, according to John, at a wedding. The wine ran out at a wedding feast in Cana. Jesus was there, and not an innocent joke was suppressed when He brought joy and grace to that special day. His mother wanted Him to use His supernatural power to make wine, thereby saving the host an excruciating embarrassment. But with utter discretion Jesus turned water into wine in such a way that the steward of the feast wondered why the best wine had been left to serve last. Only the disciples and the servants knew where it had come from (John 2:9). In performing this miracle, Jesus declared Himself to be the true source of their joy. He is the ultimate Host and the ultimate Guest.

One of the most remarkable images in the Bible is that of Jesus at His own wedding. This time He is the ultimate Groom.

In Revelation, the last book of the Bible, John inspires us with a vision of the end of the world, the Second Coming of Jesus, and the answer to our daily prayer, "Thy kingdom come on earth." The world ends not with a fizzle or a bang, but with the Second Coming of Jesus. This blessed event is described as a glorious wedding. An angel told John, "Blessed are those who are invited to the wedding supper of the Lamb" (Revelation 19:9). But there is more than a metaphor here. In some way that is too marvelous for us to comprehend, Heaven is not the end of marriage but one continuous experience of eternal marriage.

People who receive Jesus Christ in this life are not yet married to Christ. Paul speaks of our present experience of faith-relationship with Christ as *betrothal*. In the ancient world betrothal was as binding as marriage itself but did

not involve sexual consummation. It was "presexual marriage" and could only be broken by divorce. Therefore
Paul tells the believers in Corinth, "I promised you to
one husband, to Christ, so that I might present you as a
pure virgin to him" (2 Corinthians 11:2). As Christians we
have "left" other ultimate loyalties, and we cleave only to
Him. Although we are betrothed to Christ now, there is
no ultimate union with Christ in this life.

Becoming a Christian is like going to a wedding,
thinking it is someone else's, but discovering to your
exquisite joy that the whole celebration is for you. Getting
betrothed to Christ is like going to your own wedding
but discovering that this is only a dress rehearsal for the
ultimate event, an event that will be more fabulous than
eye has seen or ear heard.

So it is no wonder that Jesus is concerned with
wedding preparations (Matthew 25:1-13), with wedding
invitations (Matthew 22:1-14), and with wedding clothes
(Matthew 22:11-14; Revelation 19:7-8). And we should
be too.

What we wear to that final wedding are not the rags
of our own righteousness, but the cloak of righteousness
we don when we put ourselves into the hands of Jesus,
trusting that His death was sufficient to bring us to God
as we are. "For the wedding of the Lamb has come, and
his bride has made herself ready. Fine linen, bright and
clean, was given her to wear" (Revelation 19:7-8).

Our right to become betrothed with a view to that
wedding comes not from ourselves but from the Groom.
If someone should ask, "Can any person show any just
cause why these two persons (the sinless Christ and the
seeking sinner) may not be lawfully joined together?" not
even the Enemy can point a finger. We are not unequally
yoked. The covenant of salvation is forged of sheer grace.

The fervent and loving service that flows from it is not part of a service contract, an exchange of benefits, but unmitigated gratitude for the gift of being in an eternal covenant with the Groom.

It is the future glory of all who truly belong to Christ, the Lamb of God, to enjoy the wedding supper of the Lamb. The final dignity of the followers of Jesus is simply to be the wife of the Lamb (Revelation 21:9). That ultimate marriage inspires our marriage in this life. We will be the better wife or husband now if we want nothing greater than to be His wife then!

So, when you are sending out invitations for your wedding why not invite Jesus? He has invited you to His.